STEPHEN F.
AUSTIN

THE SON BECOMES FATHER OF TEXAS

bright sky press
HOUSTON, TEXAS

2365 Rice Boulevard, Suite 202,
Houston, Texas 77005

10 9 8 7 6 5 4 3 2 1

Library of Congress Cataloging-in Publication Data

Wade, Mary Dodson.
Stephen F. Austin : the son becomes father of Texas / by Mary Dodson Wade ;
illustrated by Pat Finney.
p. cm. -- (Texas heroes for young readers ; 6)
Includes bibliographical references and index.
ISBN 978-1-933979-45-8 (hardcover : alk. paper)
1. Austin, Stephen F. (Stephen Fuller), 1793-1836--Juvenile literature. 2. Austin, Moses
1761-1821--Juvenile literature. 3. Pioneers--Texas--Biography--Juvenile literature. 4. Texas--
History--To 1846--Juvenile literature. I. Finney, Pat, ill. II. Title. III. Series.

F389.A942W34 2009
976.4'03092--dc22
[B]   2009007859

Book and cover design by Cregan Design
Illustrations by Pat Finney
Printed in China through Asia Pacific Offset

STEPHEN F.
AUSTIN

THE SON BECOMES FATHER OF TEXAS

MARY DODSON WADE

ILLUSTRATIONS BY

PAT FINNEY

bright sky press

HOUSTON, TEXAS

TABLE OF CONTENTS

CHAPTER 1

....

Flatboat to Missouri

Five-year-old Stephen Fuller Austin climbed onto the flatboat with his mother Maria Brown Austin and his little sister Emily. He was a small, serious child with large hazel eyes and brown hair that curled in the damp breeze. Moses Austin was moving his family to Upper Louisiana, beyond the Mississippi River. Forty people were making the trip, including workers and slaves.

Maria Austin had been raised in Philadelphia by her wealthy great-uncle Benjamin Fuller. This was her second move to a wilderness home. Her husband had founded Austinville in western Virginia to mine lead

and make bullets. They had done well enough to build a big house.

Stephen, named for his father's brother and his mother's uncle, had been born there on November 3, 1793. Two years later Emily Margaret Brown Austin arrived. Now, debt forced the family to leave Austinville.

Confident that he could create another fortune, Moses Austin had traveled to a rich lead mining area near St. Louis, Missouri. His polite manners and business background impressed officials. The Spanish governor of Louisiana gave him a league of land (4428 acres) around Mine à Breton (Mine a Burton). Austin applied for Spanish citizenship and received permission to settle thirty families.

After a twisting journey on the Kanawha River the boat turned into the Ohio and ran with the swift current to the Mississippi River. Along the way accidents and illness brought tragedy. Only seventeen of their company survived to enter Spanish territory at Sainte Genevieve, about forty miles from their new home in Missouri.

Early mining practices at Mine à Breton had

been sloppy. With characteristic energy, Moses Austin made the operation profitable. He built a handsome two-story house equal to the mansions of Tidewater Virginia. Durham Hall was surrounded by a barn, stable, smokehouse, blacksmith shop, and henhouse.

Without near neighbors, Stephen often played with Shawnee Indian children. Peaceful Delaware and Shawnee came to trade at the large store his father provided for the miners. The Osage, however, were angered by settlements being built in their hunting grounds. Stephen was nine when thirty of them attacked Durham Hall before they were driven off.

Incensed over the death of a miner and the kidnapping of a woman, Moses Austin asked for soldiers to guard the mines, but the authorities refused. Moses found a three-pound cannon sunk in the muddy streets of Sainte Genevieve and got permission to haul it to the mines. He restored the cannon to working condition and placed it in front of his home.

The next year, 1803, the United States bought the vast area west of the Mississippi. The Louisiana Purchase made Missouri part of the United States. Ten-year-old Stephen watched as the American flag

was raised on the new flagpole beside Durham Hall. Each Fourth of July after that, the cannon was fired at dawn to celebrate Independence Day, and patriotic speeches filled the air.

The following year, however, Stephen was not there to hear the booming cannon. Early in the summer of 1804, even though he was not yet eleven, he set off on a thousand-mile journey to New England to go to school.

Both Moses and Maria Austin were educated. Missouri was still mostly unsettled, with no proper school for their son. Moses Austin inquired of relatives about the best place to send Stephen. The recommendation was a new academy in Colchester, Connecticut.

CHAPTER 2

Exemplary Young Man

After a long, tiresome trip filled with homesickness, Stephen settled into Bacon Academy along with 200 other boys. Nothing marked him as someone who had lived all his life far from city life. The older Austin had provided proper clothes for a gentleman's son.

A letter from his father instructed Stephen to study hard to achieve "your future greatness in life." He admonished his son to be thoughtful, but not stingy, with money. "I do not expect you will expend money unwisely. Yet I do not wish you to render yourself Disagreeable to your young friends to avoid expending a few Dollars."

In the same letter, he warned, "Your troubles on your Journey will learn you a little of what you are to expect to meet with in life." Stephen Austin as an adult would need this lesson in patience.

His studies included grammar, writing, logic, mathematics, and geography. Moses Austin wrote the headmaster a long letter concerning his son's education. He requested that Stephen learn as little Greek and Hebrew as possible. "I have thought neither of those languages of much advantage to a man of business."

Even though he expected his son to join his business enterprises, he avoided dictating what Stephen was to become. "If his talents justify I wish him for the Barr (law)." But Moses Austin did not insist on that because he had seen too many fathers push their sons into professions for which they were not suited.

He wanted his son to learn the classics, to know how to behave in polite society, to be honest, and to have "a Correct mode of thinking both Religious and Politcal...I do not wish my son [to be] a Bigot."

During his three years at the school, Stephen lived with the headmaster. When he left, Dr. John Adams handed him a certificate. "This certifies that

Stephen F. Austin has been a member of this institution. As a scholar he has been obedient and studious; as a boarder, unexceptional. Having passed the public examinations, and having during the whole period sustained a good moral character, he is judged worthy of this honorary testimonial."

Although Stephen's mother wanted him to go to Yale, he enrolled at Transylvania University in Lexington, Kentucky. During two and a half sessions there, he studied geography, math, astronomy, philosophy, and history. His dismissal certificate, dated April 4, 1810, stated that he had "conducted himself in an exemplary and praiseworthy manner."

Stephen had become a young man his parents were proud of. He was known as a person who kept his word. Reading was a passion with him. Although quiet and thoughtful, the slender young man mixed easily with everyone. He loved music and was quite a dancer. After he returned home, gossipy letters from college friends teased him about certain young ladies he had been interested in.

Although Stephen was not yet seventeen when he returned home, his father began giving him adult responsibilities at the mines and in other enterprises. With Stephen home, Maria Austin concentrated on her daughter's education. She took fifteen-year-old Emily back to New England to attend a school suitable for a family of their status. The Austins' youngest child, James Elijah Brown Austin, went along. Eight-year-old Brown was ready to begin his studies.

On their trip eastward the Austins were escorted by Elisha Lewis. Lewis had been given furs, lead, and venison hams to sell to pay their expenses. However, there never seemed to be enough money. When Maria questioned Lewis about it, he passed it off as joke. A very miffed Maria wrote her husband that Lewis "is one of those kind of men that thinks women has nothing to do with mens business."

Money problems continued to plague Maria. Nineteen-year-old Stephen was sent to New Orleans with a boatload of lead which he was to sell. He would then take the money to his mother. Unfortunately, the boat sank. Through great effort, he recovered most of the lead, but he was unable to sell it. The War of 1812 had stopped trade.

Stephen returned home, and Maria Austin

took both the children out of school. James Bryan, Moses Austin's business partner, escorted them home to Missouri. Shortly afterwards, Emily married James Bryan.

Stephen took his place in the community. He served a few months as a militia officer. He joined the Masonic Lodge. At the age of twenty-two, he was elected a member of the territorial legislature, a position he held until he left Missouri six years later.

Soon the mines began to fail. Moses Austin turned over their operation to Stephen, but he was unable to reverse the losses. Other money problems developed. The Austins lost all their money with the failure of the bank Moses Austin had helped found.

Twenty-five-year-old Stephen made an extraordinary vow to his brother-in-law. "When the day arrives that the whole family are out of Debt, I mean to *celibrate it* as my *wedding day*—which will never come untill then." Stephen Austin never married.

CHAPTER 3

....

A Father's Dream

Moses Austin refused to accept poverty. In the face of bankruptcy, he ordered wallpaper, gilt frames for his coat of arms, and a plush couch with six chairs. Finally, though, he was forced to sell Durham Hall and the lead mines. Twenty years after coming to Missouri, he had nothing, but he had no intention of giving up.

A recent treaty had made Florida part of the United States. Texas, however, remained Spanish territory. Since Spain had given him an opportunity to start over in Missouri, fifty-nine-year-old Moses Austin was sure he could do it again in Texas.

Stephen, meanwhile, had moved to Arkansas Territory and established a farm at Long Prairie on the Red River near Texas. He also bought lots in the new town of Little Rock on the Arkansas River, as well as additional land about halfway between Long Prairie and Little Rock.

The older Austin met his son in Little Rock and then set out for Texas with Stephen's slave Richmond. In his pocket he carried a copy of his Spanish passport. After a hard journey through the deserted wilderness of east Texas, he and Richmond rode into San Antonio de Béxar shortly before Christmas 1820.

Texas had been in Spanish control for over 300 years, yet there were only two settlements of any size— San Antonio and La Bahía (Goliad). Moses Austin was sure the Spanish authorities in San Antonio would see the wisdom of his plan to settle American families as a buffer against the Indians. He was unaware that the Mexican government, afraid that the United States wanted to grab Texas, had issued an order barring Americans from the country. The governor refused even to look at Moses Austin's documents and ordered him to leave immediately.

Stunned at seeing plans to recover his fortune dashed, Moses Austin started across the city plaza. By chance, he met Baron de Bastrop, someone he had known in Louisiana twenty years earlier. Bastrop, the name Philip Hendrik Nering Bögel had adopted when he fled embezzlement charges in the Netherlands, was a respected citizen in San Antonio. After hearing Austin's situation, Bastrop immediately returned to the governor and pled for his friend's request to be heard. The governor agreed to send the proposal to his superiors.

Ever confident of success, Moses Austin started home. He and Richmond survived a panther attack. Then their horses were stolen. As they walked, their powder got too damp to fire the guns. For eight days they had only roots and berries to eat. Finally, exhausted and ill, they reached a tavern twenty miles from Natchitoches (NACK-uh-tish), Louisiana. Three weeks later Moses Austin steeled himself for the return to Missouri, but Richmond was left behind, too ill to travel.

Stephen had left Long Prairie and gone to New Orleans to find a job. This proved impossible.

"I offered to hire myself as clerk, as an overseer, or anything else," he wrote his mother. "There are hundreds of young men who are glad to work for their board."

At this dark moment he met Joseph H. Hawkins, a lawyer. Hawkins gave him a place to stay, meals, and books to read. He provided money for clothes and an opportunity to study law. Stephen found work as a newspaper editor. This lasted four months, then word came that his father expected to receive a grant of land in Texas.

In Missouri, Moses Austin hurriedly settled affairs. He was ready to leave for Texas when he became ill again. Maria Austin wrote Stephen. "He called me to his bedside and with much distress and difficulty of speech, beged me to tell you to take his place…to go on with the business in the same way he would have done." Two days later, June 10, 1821, Moses Austin died.

CHAPTER 4

Anglo Settlers in Texas

Stephen Austin, unaware of his father's death, published an open letter in the newspaper inviting Americans to settle in their new colony. Then he went to Natchitoches, where Don José Erasmo Seguín waited to give the Austins a tour of Texas. His mother's letter reached him there. At the age of twenty-eight, the dutiful son assumed the responsibility of fulfilling his father's dream to recover the family fortune.

He set out immediately for San Antonio, where the governor confirmed him as heir to his father's grant. Together they worked out the arrangements to settle three hundred American families in Texas. Austin would choose a place for his colony and then prepare a map of the area for the governor.

As empresario, Austin would have complete control. He would be lawmaker, judge, jury, military leader, and land agent. He was required to collect letters of recommendation for each settler.

To his surprise the government granted more land than he had requested. Farmers got a labor (177 acres) of land. If they had cattle, even a milk cow, they got a league (4428 acres). Persons who built mills and operated other industries received extra land. Austin was responsible for keeping records of land assignments. For his work, he got extra, or premium, land which he hoped to sell to raise money.

At the end of negotiations the governor entertained his guest with a mustang hunt. The men chased bands of the small, wiry ponies over the rolling hills near San Antonio. Then, on his way out of the city, Austin viewed the efficient irrigation system that brought water from the San Antonio River to the fields around the five missions.

On his tour, Austin presented his credentials to the *alcalde* (mayor) in La Bahía. Then he explored Lavaca Bay and charted the Guadalupe, Colorado, and Brazos rivers. Three months later, he returned to Louisiana and wrote the Spanish governor that his colony would lie between the Brazos and Colorado Rivers. He praised the land on the San Marcos River as "the most beautiful I ever saw."

He returned to Natchitoches and was jubilant to find letters from a hundred eager settlers. He felt sure he could settle 1500 families, not just the original three hundred. He left immediately for New Orleans where his benefactor Hawkins provided $4000 for supplies in return for half of Austin's premium land.

In New Orleans he bought the ship *Lively* and outfitted it with tools and workers. Those on the ship were sent to the mouth of the Colorado River to build a stockade and plant corn. Unfortunately, the *Lively* entered the Brazos River rather than the Colorado. On January 1, 1822, Austin arrived with the first of his colonists. He searched for two months along the Colorado while the *Lively* settlers waited in vain for him to come.

That winter of 1821–22 was so cold that the Brazos River froze bank to bank. But three months after his arrival, Austin reported that there were fifty men on the Brazos and one hundred on the Colorado. They were building cabins and planting corn, getting ready for their families to come in the fall.

Austin's settlers had agreed to pay him twelve and a half cents per acre for the work he did as empresario. This fee covered the cost of surveying the land and the price of official paper to record the deeds. Austin allowed long periods for paying the fees because most settlers had little money. Sometimes he took cattle or pigs as payment. In the end though, most settlers paid nothing. He still counted on the sale of the premium land to restore the family's fortune.

CHAPTER 5

....

Frustrations with the Mexican Government

In order to supply the colonists with clear titles to their land, Austin went to San Antonio early in 1822. To his dismay he discovered that the original grant from the Spanish government had to be approved by a new government now that Mexico was free from Spain.

Unprepared for a long trip and fearful of leaving his colony, Austin nevertheless started for Mexico City. He and two companions traveled about a hundred miles before Comanche Indians surrounded them and took all their goods. After learning that

the men were Americans, the Indians returned everything except four blankets, a bridle, and a little Spanish grammar book. Austin had been studying the language as he rode along. When the book turned up in north Texas months later, rumors spread that Austin had been killed.

Wishing to avoid more robberies, Austin completed the journey from Monterrey to Mexico City dressed as a beggar. When he arrived, he did not know anyone and still could not speak the language. He made his appeal for confirmation, but the disorganized government made no decision. Months went by as the congress argued over rules for allowing settlers to enter.

They had almost worked out the details when Mexico's leader declared himself emperor. Congress was dismissed and more months of waiting followed as Austin started the process all over again. He lived frugally, but the $400 he had brought from Texas was soon spent. He sold his watch and then borrowed more money from Hawkins in New Orleans.

A year went by. Austin became fluent enough to make his requests in Spanish. His courteous manners impressed leaders in the capital, and influential men became his friends. Austin was determined to fulfill his duties and obligations as a Mexican citizen. At long last, the self-declared emperor approved Austin's grant.

As he prepared to return home, however, a young army officer named Antonio López de Santa Anna led a rebellion against the emperor. For the third time Austin petitioned for confirmation of his grant. His efforts were complicated by other empresarios applying for grants as well. Finally, after fifteen months of waiting, he could leave. His colony had been approved.

CHAPTER 6

....

Hardworking Empresario

Ten days after Austin returned to Texas, he established his headquarters on the high west bank of the Brazos River, about seventy miles from the Gulf of Mexico. Within three years, the village of San Felipe de Austin boasted thirty log structures. There were taverns, stores, and blacksmith shops. A two-story hotel and a newspaper office were in operation.

From his office in a double log cabin Austin directed land surveys, while Baron de Bastrop issued official land titles to settlers. Austin feared that deeds written on loose sheets might get lost, causing a

tangled mess of conflicting claims such as he had dealt with while a Missouri legislator. He bought a large book and recorded the deeds in it.

Austin neglected his own affairs as he fulfilled his duties as empresario. He personally approved each new colonist. He dealt with complaints involving stolen horses, counterfeit money, boundary disputes, missing relatives, and Indian attacks. He met with Indian delegations. To lighten his load, Austin organized districts. The district officials handled small disputes, but settlers could still appeal decisions to him.

As Austin struggled to keep up, he met Samuel May Williams, an educated New Englander who was fluent in Spanish and French. Austin liked Williams the moment he met him. He hired Williams as his secretary and paid him a large salary out of his own pocket. Williams was a tremendous help in recording the land deeds. Together the two men translated Mexican laws from Spanish to English so that the colonists could understand them.

Austin did allow himself one piece of vanity. Since he was a Mexican official, he sent to New York for a sword and a navy blue uniform with red vest and gold braid befitting his rank as army colonel.

His great joy was the company of his younger brother Brown, a high-spirited youth who had come with the first settlers. Although Austin urged the rest of his family to come, that did not happen for years. James Bryan died, leaving huge debts. Emily supported her family of four children and aging Maria Austin by teaching school and taking in boarders.

When Brown went back to Missouri to bring them to Texas, Austin sent a long letter to his mother and sister. He gave specific instructions about what to bring—seeds, dishes, beds, and the piano. He especially wanted them to bring "all the books you can." He warned them that they would live in a plain house. As for clothes, for several years "nothing should be worn in the family but homespun." Their lifestyle would "set an example to the rest of the Settlers."

Before Brown reached Missouri, though, Maria Austin died. Emily soon married James Franklin Perry, a local merchant, and Brown returned alone. Austin missed his family. The death of his friend Joseph Hawkins only deepened his sadness. The colony, however, continued to prosper.

In 1824 Mexico adopted a new constitution. It guaranteed many freedoms that Americans wanted. The only drawback was that Texas and Coahuila were combined into one state. The state capital was in Saltillo over 500 miles away, with a deputy governor for Texas residing in San Antonio.

Austin's success as empresario led to his second grant in 1825 for 500 families. In 1827 a third grant allowed 100 hundred families. The following year a fourth grant approved 300 more families. In spite of this, Austin had little money. He could not collect fees, and his premium land did not sell.

Brown married Eliza Westall, and Austin gave them large tracts of land. He helped Brown open a store in Brazoria and was overjoyed when they named their son Stephen F. Austin II. Brown's sudden death from yellow fever while on a trip to New Orleans in 1829 left Austin inconsolable.

As more American settlers came, his problems increased. They resented a government far away in Mexico telling them what to do. Haden Edwards had led a revolt in Nacogdoches (Nack-uh-DOH-chez) in 1827. Haden declared independence for the citizens of "Fredonia." Austin, the loyal Mexican citizen, led a force to put down the rebellion.

The whole affair strengthened the Mexican government's suspicions that the United States wanted to annex Texas. Alarmed over the number of settlers pouring in, the Mexican congress passed a law on April 6, 1830. No more Americans were allowed to enter Texas.

CHAPTER 7

....

Family at Last

Texans had not even heard about the law when James Perry arrived a week after its passage. Austin's brother-in-law was there to choose a place for his family. Austin picked out choice land for them near the mouth of the Brazos River. It was covered with wild peach trees. He even designed a house at Peach Point for Emily's large family. She added a few ideas of her own about the size of the rooms and the width of the back porch.

In the spring of 1831 Emily's son Moses Austin Bryan arrived before the rest of the family.

The thirteen-year-old had a sunny disposition and threw himself into learning Spanish. As he matured, he became both companion and valuable assistant to Austin. The rest of Emily's family arrived in the fall. Austin was overjoyed. Since Brown's death, the only relative he had in Texas was his namesake.

About this same time, his cousin Mary Austin Holley arrived too. The widow of a college president, she was a very attractive, talented woman. She loved books, played the guitar, and wrote songs and poetry. She had known Brown Austin because he had attended Transylvania University while her husband was president there.

She came to Texas to visit her brother Henry Austin at his place near the coast. She had published a book of her husband's writings, but she needed money. She was impressed with the beauty of the land and immediately saw the potential of a book that would let the world know about Texas. Austin made a special trip to Peach Point to meet her. He shared with her his dreams for Texas and gave her a map for the book.

She shared her cousin's interest in music, art, and

literature. He wrote his brother-in-law, "Mrs. H. is a *divine* woman." After she left, they exchanged many letters. When Mary Austin Holley published *Texas,* she dedicated the book to him.

CHAPTER 8

....

Unrest in Texas

Every year Stephen Austin expected to return to private life. He needed to build up his own affairs. Although he had land, he had no crops and no cattle he could convert to cash. Just when he thought he could retire, he was elected to the state legislature. This meant more long trips to Mexico. He was reluctant to accept this new responsibility because his health was poor. Putting aside his own wishes, he left for Saltillo. Before going, he made out a will that divided his premium land between Emily and his young namesake.

There was much unhappiness in Texas over the

law that barred American settlers. The Mexican government sent Colonel José Antonio Mexía with a squadron of six ships and four hundred men to restore Mexican control. When Austin returned to Texas from Mexico, he was on the same ship as Colonel Mexía. Austin's polite, calm manner reassured Mexía that Texas was not in revolt. Citizens in towns along the Brazos toasted the colonel. They even cheered for Santa Anna, who had vowed to support the freedoms put forth in the constitution. Colonel Mexía took his troops home.

Soon afterwards, Austin presided over a meeting at San Felipe de Austin. In the fall of 1832 delegates requested separate statehood for Texas and asked for repeal of the law forbidding more American settlers. Six months later delegates met again and wrote a state constitution for Texas.

The settlers wanted privileges such as they enjoyed in the United States—freedom of the press and the right to vote for their leaders. They also argued that Texas should be separated from Coahuila because of differences in language and culture. They wrote these requests and authorized Stephen Austin, the most logical person, to take the petition to Mexico City.

He arrived at the capital in July 1833 to find two political groups struggling for control of the government. Austin presented the petition and worked quietly during the long wait for an answer. With the help of patriot Lorenzo de Zavala, he secured repeal of the law forbidding Americans to enter Texas, but the other requests were ignored.

After months of waiting he boldly told officials that if Mexico did not let Texas become a separate state, the settlers were likely to take matters into their own hands. This infuriated Mexican officials.

Exasperated, Austin wrote a letter asking authorities in San Antonio to work out plans for a separate Texas state government. The San Antonio official read Austin's letter with alarm. It sounded like treason to him, and he sent the letter to Mexico City.

CHAPTER 9

....

Imprisoned in Mexico City

Austin had started home in December, but he was arrested in Saltillo and returned to Mexico City. He knew the Mexican trial system and wrote his brother-in-law James Perry to expect a long delay. "I may be pummeled about for a year," he said. He sent a handwritten power of attorney to his brother-in-law so that Perry could conduct any necessary land business while he was absent.

He wanted no trouble in Texas, however, and wrote his secretary Williams, "I hope there will be no excitement about my arrest. All I can be accused of is that I have labored arduously, faithfully…to have Texas made a State of the Mexican Confederation separate from Coahuila. This is all, and this is not crime."

He laid out the same defense of his actions to loyal friend Rafael Llanos, the senator from Nuevo Leon. "I have been accused of having magnificent schemes for Texas, and I confess that I have had them…It is depopulated; I wish to people it…I want the frontier protected, the lands cultivated, roads and canals opened, river navigation developed…I wish to take from my native land the best…and plant it in my adopted land."

Government officials were suspicious of his motives. On February 13, 1834, Austin was placed in the old Inquisition prison in Mexico City. For three months he sat in a dark cell thirteen feet by sixteen feet. Former prisoners had scratched scenes with snakes into the walls.

Guards pushed his food through a slot in the door. There were no windows. On clear days a shaft of light around noon time allowed enough light for reading. For a brief period each day he left solitary

confinement to go outside to get some sun, but he could not speak to anyone. During the first month even books were forbidden.

He had to provide his own food. Father Miguel Muldoon, the priest who had become his friend while serving Austin's colony, brought food and tried to get books. Finally, Austin bribed a guard and got a novel called *Yes and No*. He later received a biography of King Philip II of Spain and two volumes of Plato translated into French. Austin was greatly pleased. "I prefer bread & water with books, to the best of eating without them."

After three months he was released from solitary confinement. He was surprised to discover many educated men among his fellow prisoners.

During the eight months he was confined in three different prisons, he had little contact with Texans. They feared action on their part would make his situation worse. Austin felt abandoned. "My situation is desolate…in a prison amidst foes who are active to destroy me and forgotten at home by those I have faithfully labored to serve…I expect to die here."

Finally, two Texas lawyers arrived in Mexico

City. They carried signed statements from Texas citizens saying Austin had not planned a revolution. They explained that the Texans had asked for the constitution, and Austin had brought their petition because he spoke Spanish.

This gained Austin's release from prison on Christmas Day, but he still could not leave Mexico City. He spent time writing a thirty-page pamphlet in Spanish called "Explanation to the Public Concerning the Affairs of Texas." He wanted Mexicans to understand Texas. He worked on a project to develop a road connecting Texas, Coahuila and Chihuahua. He dreamed of goods traveling from Texas ports to Santa Fe, New Mexico.

Even though he could not leave, his spirits lifted. He attended opera and the theater. He danced at a grand ball given for the British minister. He sent home two miniature portraits. During this time he enjoyed the company of a charming young woman named Angelina Herrera, who had studied in England. He provided her tickets to see the liftoff of Mexico City's first hot air balloon. Her death during a plague was a terrible blow.

Finally, on July 11, 1835, Santa Anna issued Austin a passport to leave. Within a week he sailed for New Orleans to return to Texas after a two-year absence.

CHAPTER 10

Texas First

Austin arrived at Velasco six weeks later, and Texans erupted with joy. After spending a few precious days with Emily's family, he attended a grand celebration dinner at Jane Long's boarding house in Brazoria. Everyone waited to hear what their leader would recommend about a convention to set up a separate government. Austin spoke clearly, "Texas needs peace, and a local government."

Returning to San Felipe, he found his house in shambles and wrote to his brother-in-law. "I want a barrel of beef...two beds and bedding...some spoons—some rice—some beans…I want a brick layer to build the kitchen chimney, which has fallen down…I hardly know what I want…Show this to the ladies, and among you fit me out with something."

Within the week, he wrote delegates urging them to attend a consultation to organize Texas under the Constitution of 1824. They were to bring a list of men and military supplies available in their district, just in case war resulted.

When he learned General Martín Perfecto Cós was advancing into Texas with a large army, Stephen Austin sent a second circular. The man who had for years so patiently counseled peace, spoke strong words, "WAR is our only recourse."

A company of Mexican soldiers appeared at Gonzales and demanded cannon that the government had given the settlers to fight off Indians. The Texans refused. After a skirmish, the soldiers retreated to San Antonio. Austin rode through the rain to Gonzales. There he reluctantly accepted the role of commander-in-chief.

He marched the troops to San Antonio. Along the way, Ben Milam, who had just escaped from a Mexican jail, joined them. Then Juan Seguín rode into camp with thirty-seven Tejano volunteers. Born in Texas, they provided invaluable assistance as scouts. Before any battle took place, though, the Consultation called Austin back for a different duty.

After Austin left San Antonio, the Texans stormed into the city. Ben Milam was killed, but Cós surrendered and marched his army back to Mexico. Texans were sure they had won their freedom. No one suspected that General Santa Anna was marching north with 3000 men.

Stephen Austin was not in Texas during its darkest hours. A few days after Christmas 1835, the Consultation sent him and two other men to the United States. These commissioners were seeking loans to pay for war with Mexico.

While they were making their way to important cities in the United States, delegates meeting at Washington-on-the-Brazos on March 2, 1836, signed the Texas Declaration of Independence. Four days later the Alamo fell, but Austin and the others did not hear about it for weeks. On March 7 Austin spoke to a large crowd in Louisville, Kentucky. He urged them to send aid and volunteers to promote "the great cause of liberty."

He paid a brief but welcome visit to Mary Austin Holley in Lexington. He gave her a copy of his Louisville speech, with permission to print it in the new edition of her book about Texas. From there, he joined the other two commissioners in New York City. Terrible news concerning the Alamo reached them there. They learned of desperate citizens fleeing with the retreating Texas army. "My heart and soul are sick," said Austin, "but my spirit is unbroken."

After meetings in Washington, D.C. and Baltimore, Maryland, Austin started home. Along the way he received the joyous news of General Sam Houston's victory at San Jacinto on April 21, 1836.

Two months after the battle that freed Texas, Austin was back in Texas. Friends urged him to run for the presidency of the new republic. Who, they asked, was better qualified to guide the country than the man who had done so much for Texas?

The same newspaper that outlined Austin's qualifications carried an advertisement for Sam Houston as president. Austin knew he would not win over the wildly popular Hero of San Jacinto, but it did not matter to him. All he longed for was time to spend on his own affairs. Three days before the election, he wrote his brother-in-law to build him a cabin at Peach Point and order furniture for it from New Orleans.

Sam Houston won almost every vote in the election. Without hesitation, the new president chose as Secretary of State the man most qualified to help the new Republic of Texas—Stephen Fuller Austin.

Austin's health was very bad, but he put Texas first. He rented a room in Columbia, about fifteen miles from Peach Point. Long into the night, he worked in the barn-like building that served as capitol. Sitting on a rawhide chair in the flickering candlelight, he wrote instructions to ministers and envoys. Above everything else, Texas must be recognized as a country by other nations. The place he loved, where he had spent his adult life faithfully looking out for its interests, could not survive unless other countries accepted it as a nation independent from Mexico.

Even as he worked, Austin planned improvements to the place he called home. In late December he sent rose cuttings and seeds to James Perry. He explained the value that well-kept shrubbery added to property.

As 1836 drew to a close, forty-three-year-old Austin became desperately ill with pneumonia. Doctors argued over treatment. Two days after Christmas a norther blew in. He lay shivering on a pallet in front of the fireplace in Judge McKinstry's house in Columbia.

For fifteen years, Stephen Fuller Austin had given his life to Texas. It was in his thoughts at the end. Delirious, he roused up and said, "Texas recognized. Archer told me so. Did you see it in the Papers?"

The following day President Houston sent out the sad announcement, "The Father of Texas is no more!" At the announcement of Austin's death on December 27, 1836, honor guards marched overnight to the Perry house. The body of Stephen Fuller Austin was placed aboard the steamer *Yellowstone* and taken down the Brazos River to Peach Point. He was buried with honors in the family cemetery, home at last.

TIMELINE

1793	November 3, born in Austinville, Virginia
1797	Moves family to Upper Louisiana (Missouri)
1804	Enters Bacon Academy, Colchester CT
1810	Graduates Transylvania University, Lexington, KY
1812	Helps father run lead mines
1815	Elected to Missouri Territory legislature
1818	Director Bank of St. Louis
1819	Goes to Long Prairie, Arkansas Territory
1820	Moses Austin goes to Texas to seek grant
1821	Moses Austin dies; becomes empresario
1823	Receives permission to settle 300 families
1826	Fredonian Rebellion
1830	Americans forbidden to enter Texas
1831	Emily Perry's family moves to Texas
1831	Mary Austin Holley visits Texas
1833	Takes petition to Mexico; arrested and imprisoned
1835	Returns to Texas; sent to United State to seek aid
1836	December 27, dies in Columbia

AUTHOR'S NOTE

In 1910 Stephen F. Austin's remains was moved to the state cemetery in Austin. Monuments honoring him can be found at Stephen F. Austin State University in Nacogdoches and at the site of San Felipe de Austin. Elisabet Ney's statue of Austin, a copy of the one in Statuary Hall in Washington, D.C., is in the Texas capitol. A giant statue stands beside State Highway 35 in Angleton. But one of his best monuments is in the General Land Office—the huge book listing grants to his original colonists.

Emily Bryan Perry carefully placed all of her brother's papers in the little office beside her house. She died in 1851. Her children were prominent in Texas. William Joel Bryan founded the city of Bryan. Moses Austin Bryan was present to translate at the meeting between Houston and Santa Anna on the San Jacinto battlefield. Guy M. Bryan, a founding member of the Texas State Historical Association, preserved the Austin papers, and his children gave them to the University of Texas. When printed, they filled 3000 pages.

Perry descendants continue to live at Peach Point in West Columbia. Austin's little office and all but two rooms of Emily's house were destroyed by a hurricane in 1909. The surviving rooms have been restored as a small museum.

Austin's namesake died at the age of ten, not many months after his uncle. A lawsuit upheld his mother's claim to the land her son inherited.

Joseph Hawkins died in poverty, but his heirs received their share of the premium lands.

A few months after seeing Stephen Austin in Louisville, Mary Austin Holley talked with Santa Anna as he traveled to Washington to meet with the American president. At Austin's death, she composed a poem that honored his selfless work for Texas. She never moved to the Texas land Austin willed to her and died of yellow fever in New Orleans in 1846. Her obituary spoke of her accomplishments in literature, her insightful mind, and her forceful personality.

It was Austin's wish to build a great university near the center of the state. The main campus of the University of Texas is located in the city which bears his name.

SOURCES

Note: The quotations have original spellings.

"your future…"; rest of paragraph and the next. Moses Austin to Stephen Austin, December 16, 1804, *The Austin Papers*, edited by Eugene C. Barker, published in three volumes by the U.S. Government Printing Office and the University of Texas, I, 93.

"I have thought…" and rest of paragraph. Moses Austin to [headmaster, supposedly, fall of 1804] *Austin Papers*, I, 95

"This certifies that…" Certificate of Scholarship and Conduct, January 7, 1808, *Austin Papers*, I, 144.

"conducted himself…" Certificate of Attendance at Transylvania University, April 4, 1810, *Austin Papers*, I, 171.

"is one of…" Maria Austin to Moses Austin, July 29, 1811. manuscript, Austin Papers, University of Texas.

"When the day…" Stephen F. Austin to James Bryan, December 31, 1818, *Austin Papers*, I, 335.

"I offered…" and rest of paragraph. Stephen F. Austin to Maria Austin, January 20, 1821, *Austin Papers*, I, 373.

"He called me…" Maria Austin to Stephen F. Austin, June 8, 1821, *Austin Papers*, I, 395.

"the most beautiful…" "Journal of Stephen F. Austin on His First Trip to Texas, 1821" *Quarterly of the Texas State Historical Association* 7 (April 1904), 296.

"all the books…" and rest of paragraph. Stephen F. Austin to Maria Austin and Emily Bryan, May 14, 1824, *Austin Papers*, I, 784-787.

"Mrs. H. is…" Stephen F. Austin to James Perry, December 27, 1831. *Austin Papers*, II, 726.

"I may be…"Stephen F. Austin to James Perry, January 12, 1834, in Eugene C. Barker, *The Life of Stephen F. Austin, Founder of Texas, 1793-1836* (Austin: The Texas State Historical Association, 1925, reprint 1949), 376.

"I hope there will…" Stephen F. Austin to Samuel M. Williams, January 12, 1834, *Austin Papers*, II, 1024.

"I have been accused…" Stephen F. Austin to Rafael Llanos, January 14, 1834, as quoted in *Life of Stephen F. Austin*, 377.

"I prefer bread…" "The 'Prison Journal' of Stephen F. Austin," ed. W. P. Zuber, *Quarterly of the Texas State Historical Association* 2 (January 1899), 201.

"My situation…"Stephen F. Austin to Samuel M. Williams, October 6, 1834, *Austin Papers*, III, 7.

"Texas needs peace…" Stephen F. Austin to the People of Texas, September 8, 1835, *Austin Papers*, III, 116-119.

"I want…" Stephen F. Austin to James Perry, September 9, 1835, *Austin Papers*, III, 121.

"WAR is our…" Stephen F. Austin to Columbia Committee, September 19, 1835, *Austin Papers*, III, 129.

"the great cause…" Austin speech, Louisville, Kentucky, March 7, 1836, as printed in Mary Austin Holley, *Texas* (Lexington, Kentucky: J. Clarke and Company, 1836) facsimile reprint Texas State Historical Association, 1985, 280.

"My heart and soul…" Stephen F. Austin to William Bryan, April 24, 1836, *Austin Papers*, III, 340.

"Texas recognized…" George L. Hammeken, "Recollections of Stephen F. Austin," *Southwestern Historical Quarterly* 20 (April 1917), 380.
Note: A slightly different wording of this, recorded by Austin's nephew who was also there when he died, is found in Moses Austin Bryan, "Personal Recollections of Stephen F. Austin," *Texas Magazine* 3 (September and November, 1897) 2: 171-172.

"The Father of Texas…" Sam Houston, "General Orders Concerning Austin's Death, December 27, 1836," *Writings of Sam Houston*, vol. II, Amelia W. Williams and Eugene C. Barker, eds. (Austin: University of Texas Press, 1941), 28.

INDEX